# Widow's Walk
## From Vietnam Veteran to Now

Pam Slate

# Forward

Whether you are prepared for this next chapter in life or not you will find that the spectrum of emotions by far are more than just grief. Questions will keep you up at night on decisions from finance to life itself. This will invade the depths of your every thought. Who do I call first? How am I going to go on? How am I going to pay the bills? Why Lord, Why? I am so mad at you Lord! What am I supposed to do, here alone? What is my purpose to go on? How do I sleep without you? Is that you…..talking to me from…there?

Let me assure you all of this will pass.

The old adage time heals all wounds is true in many ways. Though it may heal the surface the deepest point in your soul will always feel it. I truly believe when you lose your partner and do so how mine left, and coupled with the next month's events I had to live through, you develop a form of PTSD. To this day I have flashbacks of that morning, things I remember vividly of that first week and the ensuing months that came all too quickly.

In this book in order for the reader to have the understanding it had to be written for those who have not had to walk this path. I felt the need to run through the timeline of my life from that fatal day as well as events that caused that day. Then we will stroll together through the remembrance and the night of awakening, and the purpose revealed. I hope my journey will ease or at least help with someone else's walk on this path in life. Or help prepare someone else for the future.

And so the next chapter of life began.

ISBN:1719016828
ISBN-13:9781719016827

# DEDICATION

This book is dedicated to my two sons and daughter in law, without you I could not have made it through.

# CONTENTS

# ACKNOWLEDGMENTS

I would like to acknowledge my attorney who helped me tirelessly that first year.

I would like to acknowledge the oncologist who talked to me on his level and did not leave me out of decisions within our control.

I would like to acknowledge my boss at this time who, was so understanding of the situation I was living in.  His selflessness & help gave me the financial strength during John's illness.

And finally to my Dad who many times drove down to take John to his appointments in Temple.

# CHAPTER ONE-THE DAY MY LIFE CHANGED FOREVER

April 15, 2006 had begun with me being awakened to the darkness before the dawn. At about 3am I was startled awake by a way of breathing from my husband John that I had never heard before. In retrospect I knew in my soul what was happening. But at the time my mind didn't connect to the soul.

During John's illness I had laid awake listening to him sleeping many nights. I would hear how his breath would sound easy and peaceful or not. But this morning was something out of the norm by far. He was making a kind of gurgle/gasp noise and audibly saying "NO" between each breath. The week before, the hospice nurse and the oncologist had told me the end was very near. Their analogy of how things would go down was more peaceful, and serene like going to sleep and never waking up. They did not prepare me for this!

I got out of bed and walked around to his side of the bed to try to assess what was happening. He was cool to the touch, his lips a shade of blueish purple. I could determine the noise I was hearing wasn't choking, but was that he was in some form of distress, as far as I understood. His eyes were open and when I initially touched his face he turned his face towards me, all the while still going through what he was going through. His eyes were fixed on my every move. He was pleading; it felt like from some deep place.

I picked up the phone and dialed the hospice nurse. No answer. I then dialed the VA Oncology Department at the Temple VA Hospital where his Dr. was supposed to have staff 24/7. No answer. Both phones just rang and rang. Both the nurse and the Dr. had given me direct lines to call if I needed anything, and for when the time came. I was instructed to use this line even if had any questions or just needed care advice. I had been assured someone would be there 24/7. Here I was, over 100 miles from the VA Medical Center where he had been treated, and near 40 miles to the nearest hospital. So calling 911 was a waste of resources in my mind.

I dialed the hospice nurse again and an answering service picked up, they assured me the nurse would return my call immediately. She did call, I think it was immediately, but cannot really say with certainty. On that morning it seemed like an eternity had passed before I received a call from her. During that time fretting over him, and my mind going wild it seemed like no one cared and we were out there alone…to die! I was holding my composure for him but the will was weakening fast, or so it felt.

When the hospice nurse finally called I briefed her on when the unusual breathing started and then held the phone where she could hear what was going on with his breathing. She advised me to crush a morphine pill up into a small amount of honey and put under his tongue and she would be headed my way. The liquid morphine the oncologist had ordered two weeks before still had not been shipped from the VA Pharmacy only 60 miles away. Understand the reason I say this now, because when end of life is near the best a caregiver can do is to keep the loved one out of pain and comfortable. This is the time when all medical intervention is over.

The nurse said she only lived a few miles away and before we hung up and after the morphine was given she asked me to take the phone to another room and listen to her. She advised the end was here. His body was shutting down. The breathing was what is called the death breath.

After I hung up with her I went to his side of the bed eased down near him and held him in my arms with tears flowing and held him for the next four and half hours alone, just him and me until he released his last breath at 8:15am. No one ever came during that time it was just me and my husband in our bedroom one last time.

I knew the moment he was gone from this life because not only did his body go limp, the air in the room from that very moment he left was different. A hush ensued but not really a peaceful quiet, just a quiet. The hospice nurse arrived at 10:30am.

Once I was sure he was at peace I started the phone call to family and friends until the nurse and others could arrive. My family drove in from over 80 miles away and arrived before the nurse did. The funeral home arrived minutes behind her.

Honestly I think I just called my parents and sons because to this day I do not remember calling the funeral home or anyone else. I do remember by very soon after daylight my small house was filled with people. My first real memory was of the funeral director and son when they were taking his drape covered body past me in the living room headed for the door.

I remember John's dog "Hubert G. Dog, aka Sargent Major Meathead" (a Bass-adore) began a forlorn howl that he had never done before. at that moment the body went by the door, I think Hubert knew too!

One other thing I clearly remember about how I felt then, is though the house was full of people doing their best to help, I felt like was I behind a bubble or glass if you will, alone, looking out into the fog of people. Have you ever felt alone in a crowd? I did that day. It was a similar feeling I felt the day of my Grandfathers funeral 30 years before when we were back at the house and the entire community was there eating, talking and remembering.

Everyone left before dark the day he was taken away and that evening and that night seemed to go on forever. You would think a caregiver would collapse and rest after all that I had been through for the past 3 years and certainly the last few months and weeks. A person with the grace and passion in their sole to truly care for another human tirelessly for months, understands where I was. This night's sleep would not come easily. On this night my mind didn't agree with my body's needs. I am typically an over-planner and over-thinker; therefore when put in a situation out of my comfort zone and control my mind goes into overdrive. Typical "Leo" women…will try to be in charge where no charge can be found!

A few nights before his death I was having another mind over body experience again where sleep wasn't going to happen so I had sat down in my favorite chair and prepared a list of who needed to be contacted, their addresses and phone numbers. All the while I sat there with the TV on not hearing a thing except for my mind screaming from within and the feeling of the grief smothering me. Remember at this time I was the only one in our marriage that knew of the perceived events that were about to unfold. Knowing was no comfort and knowing did little for me at 3 am that Saturday morning. While doing this list I did not know that next few months to year would be a roller coaster of emotional turmoil. I remember the anger at God for taking my love, my husband, my rock from me too early. Isn't a happy, loving, marriage, relationship what we are supposed to embrace in this life? Isn't this the Lord's command for us? My thoughts would travel down the road of "Why the heck would the Lord do this or allow it?" "Why didn't he heal him as I had diligently prayed for, for months? " I faithfully laid hands as you directed me O Lord",( not a typical response for a person brought up in a VERY conservative belief) "My God have you forsaken me?" "Why would you make your child so unhappy?" Morning dawned, no sleep at about the time the phone started ringing. Argh!

The next morning started with the first call coming in from the funeral home. They needed me to come to the office to sign papers, bring financial information and make some decisions. Since John had served in the US Marine Corp he wanted a military style funeral and to be buried next to his first wife near the family plot in Ft Worth Texas area. When I hung up from the funeral home I walked to the closet to retrieve his Vietnam Era USMC dress uniform from the zippered bag to take with me to the funeral home. While getting it out the second call came in. This call was from my dad, mom & sister to say they were on their way back down and to wait for them they would go with me to the funeral home. No one but me knew I had already made most of the decisions the Tuesday before. I didn't know why that Tuesday I had drove to the funeral home alone but I did.

I carefully chose a casket with American Eagles with the American Flag inset on each corner, the USMC Logo embroidered inside the lid, set up the Marine Corp personnel to fold the flag and play taps, picked out the vault the casket would be buried in, flowers that would be there, and how I was going to pay for all this!. Looking back I really think God's hand guided me there on Tuesday before his death to help take some burden off me later.

While waiting for my parents and sister to arrive I opened the uniform bag and saw that his dress blues were in bad shape. The years of hanging in the zippered travel bag did them no favors. There were moth holes throughout the wool suite, the normally starch white gloves and cap had yellowed, and his ribbons and medals were missing. Eighteen years of his life ruined. OMG! What was I going to do? I didn't have the money, contacts or time to recreate this uniform and to fill his wishes. I had to take charge and make a very unsavory tough decision, all the while telling myself to calm down and breathe!

Family started arriving around 10 am, so they said, and from there all I remember of this day are some things Dad said from and to the funeral home director's office. I really don't remember the drive to the funeral home or back to the house. The family has told me stories of the day and what happened with neighbors and such.

Let me set the scene. We lived on a 6+ acre tract of land our house was at the back edge of the tract off the road. To come into our front yard a person would have to travel up a gravel drive. The story goes that one of my neighbors on an adjoining tract of land who we had had trouble with when we first bought the tract, brought his grandson and the child's kite and stood in our front yard looking towards the house while the kid flew his kite. A normal person would have at least come to the door and inquired instead of standing in the front yard gawking like a fool. This neighbor ended up being a bigger problem after John was gone. I guess he lacked the manners and etiquette training growing up to know better or was just that rude.

I am going to change direction here to fill in more gaps of the story that became my walk as a widow. John's dad had a small mobile home on our property where he had lived near us. His dad died December 27, 2015 just 3 ½ months before John died. The family during this three month period had done nothing to probate his dad's estate, deal with this house that had a loan on it, remove any assets etc. And I was still processing this closed chapter of my life when John died! No rest for the weary was right!

The day came for the funeral, Thursday after he had died. Family and friends previous coworkers traveled from out of state and locally and arrived at the graveside ceremony. Some of these people I to this day did and do not know. The graveside was filled with flowers, family and friends just like he wanted. The Marines were there in their dress blues. But John wasn't wearing his. That hard decision I spoke of earlier was to place him to rest in his dress suite. He did keep his USMC Ring on. The flowers were overwhelming beautiful. And I mention this because John loved flowers.

About three or four weeks before he died we were setting in the living room and from out of the blue he said "Do you think I will have flowers at my funeral ?" A tough Veteran Marine, worrying about flowers at his own funeral! He loved flowers. Even though his Marine tough personality is what most people saw he still was tender at heart about flowers!

When he asked this no one had told him with certainty he was close to death. I would not allow it! I do not to this day think it is fair to tell a person a time line of death. The depression that overtook him when he found out he was going to die only lasted for 4 days until he was dead. It is cruel to burden a person that is sick with all the "what ifs" that go along with knowing. It is also cruel for a person to be stripped of hope of life.

He had already expressed his wishes of a Military style funeral and this thought of flowers took me by surprise to a point. So his thoughts were to be sent to the next life with the things he truly loved, the Marine brothers at his side and a presentation of beautiful flowers surrounding his body and casket.

If you have never had the "pleasure" to spend your life with a Vietnam era Marine and see the many facets of the soft side fight with the "Marine" personality you haven't lived! John was a Camel Smoking, Bud Drinking, proud, and angry from somewhere deep within, macho Marine for his outward persona. But as his wife I knew the other side that would not be allowed to be seen often. He was the one that would cry at a sappy movie, or a puppy that was hurt. He was also the softness that could clear the tears and fears of our granddaughter. At the end John wanted the simple assurance of leaving this old world surrounded by who he loved and what he loved.

The funeral started with "dearly beloved we are gathered here to celebrate the life of......" then went onto the Marines removing the flag from on top of his casket, folding it carefully and kneeling on one knee in front of me to thank me for his service to his country and fellow man by paying the ultimate price with his life. I lost it when I clutched the flag to my chest. Tears of grief coupled by uncontrolled embarrassing sinus noises left me broken and embarrassed. It took a bit to regain my composure. Somewhere between the first sounds of the lone bugler playing taps to the first person from the crowd walking up to the now open casket to pay their respects. He did not die in the line of duty he died from diseases that were directly related to chemicals used in Vietnam during his time of duty.

At 46 years old this is not where you ever could have envisioned being. But here I was. At that moment of conscious awareness I could have just started screaming uncontrollably. But my southern heritage and Leo mentality kept me in check for now.

Once the crowd had started to depart I remember standing at the casket, petting his hair, trying my hardest not to lose it again.

And as I walked away from the casket I remember overhearing John's brother say "I am tired of coming to Texas to bury people." I thought to myself what a selfish rude person. He never once offered his condolences or concern for my needs. I don't believe he even spoke to me at all that day. Dusty, the brother, and one of their Dad's sisters were the only extended family John had at his funeral.. His mother and sister did however come by train a few months after this to a family reunion in Ft. Worth. But she didn't come to her own sons funeral ?!

Dusty popped in makes a scene then leaves! I really didn't understand how his brother would turn till the upcoming months.

The day finally came to a close me setting at the house alone, going over what part of my life that was now gone and what was to be in the future.

# CHAPTER 2-THE VA MEDICAL ATROCITIES & HOW WE ARRIVED TO THAT DAY

Through the VA Medical system I have witnessed atrocities from lack of care to over abuse of medications and test. I have even witnessed sign ups to use our Veterans like test animals on new procedures. It makes me sick what I witnessed those 13 days John was in the hospital, before his death.

Two weeks before John left this life he was in the Temple VA Medical Hospital due to complications from the chemotherapy he had received. This treatment would usually leave him with a critical diminished mental state. He would start talking to the dead, hallucinating or sleeping so soundly without wanting to eat, drink or any other body functions. John had begged for these treatments on hope of a cure. The VA was not going to proceed with treatment of Mastitis Liver and Kidney Cancer at stage IV.

At this time his red blood cell count was usually critical, unless he had just received a transfusion and within hours of the "chemo" his white blood cell count would drop to a critically low point. I look back and over the 3 months he received "chemo" he never lost his hair, he never had any of the other side effects of "chemotherapy". Was he actually getting chemo? Or was it some other drug that took his life quicker? The oncologist had said it was dangerous and futile to treat him early on, but John begged him to at least try. Should a Veteran have to beg for medical care?

Let me back up a little, John and I had spent 3 years of going to the various VA Medical Facilities through countless test, blood draws and such before he was diagnosed. His arms looked like a very bruised pin cushion, not counting the bone marrow test (with no pain meds, or anesthesia. By the time he was actually diagnosed he was stage IV. It took 3 years because the appointments didn't come right away. We had to set up the appointment sometimes more than three months out to get a spot to be seen. He was shuffled from one team to another, (like green team to red team) often. Our visits usually entailed driving to the Temple Facility or Waco Tx which meant 60-100 miles away. The multiple years of chasing appointments, starting over with new Dr.'s as the VA rotated in the "new class", files being lost, and it gave us both a sense of the system being more than broken. The staff had no compassion to our pleading for help as long as they received their paycheck we felt like they could care less. This allowed his cancer to grow rapidly without treatment. Secondary cancer is bad but let untreated guarantees death!

John's last 13 days in the Temple VA Hospital was long and hard on me as his caregiver. I stayed with him 24/7 until the Monday before he went home. He had a reaction to the "chemo" and he went from the treatment room to being admitted. He was weak, hallucinating, trying to urinate but couldn't, talking to the dead and more. To see him this way after every treatment had become our norm, but this one was extremely violent.

The entire 13 days we were there the staff did not offer one time to bath him, not one time help clean him or change is throw away underwear, even when he would soil himself. Not one time did they offer to change or even help with his bed linens. It was so bad, I learned the key pad code to the linen closet, and to the cleaning supplies closet so I could do their job. Even when I asked for help, I didn't get it. I am not a frail small person but picking up another adult human alone requires a lot more muscle strength than the norm. I knew in my soul I had to stay there to insure shots were given, his medication given and just respectable care. I had to remind them many times to just bring him his food!

Monday April 10th he had shown a little improvement after his 7th blood transfusion and was somewhat cognitive. I really needed to go to the house wash clothes and catch up a little bit. I met with the Oncologist that morning why John was eating breakfast. The Dr. told me the end was very near and begged me to let him stay at the hospital for many reasons. He was sure the hour was very close. I spoke to me him about the lack of care and received a personal promise from him to me, that John would receive his rightful care if I needed to go home that day. I agreed and took him at his word as long as he promised me the *NO ONE* would tell John that he was at death's door. He assured me staff would be on point and I should go home and rest. John and I spoke about it and I finally agreed to go home that evening and planned on coming back the early the next morning.

Tuesday morning was the day I was led to stop by the funeral home on my way back to the hospital. I guess this was God's way of preparing me for the weekend that was coming.

I went through the very hard process of picking out a casket, vault and other things needed to insure his funeral was planned per his wishes. The 100 miles back to the hospital seemed longer with my mind in overdrive with worry and trying to drive.

When I arrived back at the hospital and then to John's room he was setting on the side of the bed crying uncontrollably. He was alone. My Marine was broken deep within his being. I sat down next to him to try and calm him down to determine what was wrong. I found out that his regular oncologist was off duty that day and the floor "shift" Dr. had took it upon himself to go around the oncologist orders and my request. John had been told by this "Dr." he was dying and they were not offering him anymore medical care. He went on to say he had been released from the hospital to go home to die.

Up to now John had hope of recovery. Now he knew he was near death's door. His demeanor after that and when he was lucid was that of a deeply depressed man with no hope. He died the Saturday after he had been told.

I was so angry at the VA "staff", and I can tell you for sure the staff at the nurses station understood me clearly! I went back to John's room told him I was taking him home and I would be filing a complaint on all of them. I cleaned him up, changed him into fresh lounging pants, t-shirt and slippers. I then picked him up, placed him in the wheelchair grabbed his personal belongings from around the room, handed him his flowers and balloons that had been sent to him and out of that hospital we went. I did not stop again at the nurses station or oncologist office and wheeled him right past the idiot "Dr." No one approached me as we left. My husband was going with me!

The ride home was very quiet with him sleeping most of the way. I can tell you with full certainty from that day forward he would not eat much or even drink much. By Thursday he slept around the clock. Saturday he left this old world, not peacefully as I hoped. I always kidded around saying he died on April 15th as his last act of defiance to the IRS. This was the government entity that he loathed the most.

# CHAPTER THREE: UNDERSTANDING THE FRAME OF MIND

I want to reveal a little insight into me to help you understand some of why I do, what I do. And please understand after an event like this in your life, you are never the same person, again. Something changes you deep within.

As a caregiver, bread winner, and wife I was not only making day to day life decisions for me but life altering decisions for John. His blood cell counts were so low continually, unless he just was hours after a transfusion, which he received 7 from January to April. His frame of mind could go from being in one day talking to the dead or the next day quoting law. A side note to his normal was, when he was drafted he was a 3rd year law student. Therefore during his illness, I just never knew what to expect from him. We often woke each morning to a new world on his mind.

The next chapter expectation facts were laid out before me by a close friend of John's who was also a Vietnam Veteran and an attorney. He, at the time was an estate attorney and his advice helped me take on the next few steps and months a little easier. I cannot say enough about how I appreciated him. There were many panic calls from law suit notices received from the "brother" during the first year. This attorney friend helped me file the probate for John's estate all the while defending me from John's brother and family over his Dad's estate.

Within a month of John's death the brother started suing me over the Dad's mobile home, contents and other things on my property. These suits kept coming like a barrage of bullets over the next 8 months! It was like a bad dream you just cannot shake yourself awake from. Every time there was a lull, my mind started stressing over what was coming next. I had become gun shy, per say. I was trying to grow out of my grief stricken state yet to be jerked back every turn by his brother and "the neighbor".

The first filing as I remember was over the 100's of 1/24th scale model cars his dad had in his mobile home. OMG, I did not want them, or even desire them. I have never been materialistic. The second filing was over him trying to force me to pay for the mobile home mortgage. Mind you, all of this was before and during him filing probate on his Dad's estate. John's dad had a will as he had told us, but my attorney and I could never find a copy. The will had left most everything to John. The will had been redone by his Dad's attorney because of near the last of his life, John and I were the only family that would take him in, care for him without using him. I still to this day believe the brother found the will and destroyed it for his own gain. But in the end, he has a bigger judge to answer to.

The next filing was over him wanting a trailer the Dad had made from the bed of a Toyota pickup. It was nothing of value; it had a bad hitch, bald tires and had been setting holding hundreds of broken bricks for years. All he had to do is come get it! The fourth demand was his attempt for me to relinquish my rights to John's part of his Dad's estate. That was the last suit I remember and in his zeal to try to hurt me, he neglected to notice he signed over his and his sisters heir-ship to me for the house his Dad and estranged wife owned in El Paso, TX. Greed is a two edged sword, isn't it?

Now, I was usually very pragmatic in how I looked at life. I was usually thorough on things to a point of excess. I had already arranged our Wills, Directives, Life Insurance Policies and other legal papers including his DD214 in one folder. Thank God I did this. This made the next task so much easier. Though it made the task easier it did not remove the anxiety of what life was to bring.

The second month after this life altering event I was having one of my sleepless nights and started researching my rights or even benefits as a widow. I was seeking any financial help, guidance or assurance I could find. I found the Social Security Death Benefit form, printed and mailed it. I found the VA Survivors form for widows of persons with service connected disabilities. I printed it, gathered documents and had it in the mail the next day. The week I sent this filing off something very strange started happening. I started receiving calls from other attorneys that wanted to represent me in a Federal Torte Suits against the Temple VA Medical Center and staff for their neglect of John's medical care. I knew their medical care and such was very lacking at best. And I thought to myself, "Hmm,"What is this was about".

One of the attorney's I spoke with ask that why I was considering her suggestions that I was to go to the VA Medical Facility Records Clerk and have them print for me every last page of his records. She said this had to be done immediately and before they changed the records. I guess the VA on a death changes records that might reflect questionable care? Hmmm. This just gave me more things to keep me up nights worrying over.

I did what she said and 600+ pages later I had his medical care records printed and in my hands. I should have listened to their advice and let them pursue that avenue, but my attorney friend advised me that it would not change the system. Of course I would be financially set about ten years down the road but did I want to live the trauma that long? I Iindsight, I should have made a stand then when the opportunity presented itself. At least I would have been on record for the neglect and illegal excuse of medical care given to our Veterans.

A very unusual thing happened after those calls or so I thought. It only took 14 days from the day I mailed the widows pension compensation forms to the VA before I received my first deposit. No government entity especially the VA works that quickly on claims of benefits! I have never witnessed any Veteran receive approval that fast. You can only imagine what I was thinking!

As a stable thinker and doer as I thought I was, I remember one afternoon about July 2006. I was driving out Interstate 30 East and I had a financial thought revelation. The attorney friends fees were starting to eat up what was left of the life insurance money, and an anxiety attack came over me, which I wasn't use to, to the point I had to pull off into a rest area and calm down. My thoughts were I was going to lose everything we had worked so hard for! The attorney fees alone to that day were over $4800.00. The life insurance was only 50K and after the funeral home cost of near 13k, catching up the bills, paying off some of the smaller bills, my safety net was dwindling fast. Every step I took closing out his life and moving on in mine cost me some fee. All the certified copies of the Death Certificate from the state, I could just here the state registers ring cha ching. The fees to close, re-file, change name, change title, etc. we're adding up more in others coffers and depleting mine.

Then one day I was off work so I thought I would do the right thing and go to the bank to change the account to just my name. WRONG! This was our joint account that I had deposited the insurance money into and that my monthly paycheck was going into via direct deposit.

His estate had not final probated yet so the bank person, with no regards to my plight, put a freeze on the account. I was penniless in an instant! All because of another's self-serving non caring human action. Nothing I could do, present or provide would make that bank change their mind. Death Certificate did not help; Letter of Testamentary filing of probate, copy of will, did not help!

I walked out so mad, frustrated, lost, betrayed, and worried. So here goes my mind again on overdrive. I had to call HR and get the auto deposits stopped; I had to get money to open a different account so I could live. Until they were presented with the finalized probate, a month or so later, my money sat there in their hands. And being presented with a final probate did not make them immediately release the account. Multiple trips later, a call from my attorney to the branch manager and another trip up there I received my money and closed the account. I look back now and know that their self-serving actions were illegal. Proof the balance in that account was my funds deposited after his death and before from the life insurance proceeds let alone the direct deposit of my payroll earnings should have been enough.

I advise any widow with a joint account where there are no other heirs to the funds draw out the funds, or transfer them out of the joint account before bank is made aware of death. Better yet, just take your money and open another account at a different bank in your name only and deposit there. DO NOT deposit in an existing Joint Account!

By this time the nightmares of his last breath and events still played like a horror movie in my mind day in and day out. I look back and surmise the stress of that date was haunting me in ways I didn't know. I started having a few health issues, my weight started climbing and so on.

Back to me being pragmatic is what helped me survive. I know this in my soul. That first year and the events of that year have changed me dramatically deep within forever.

Remember me asking the Lord why? Also the anger at the Lord, etc... Whether you are a faith believer or not this walk will draw you to your almighty's loving arms. You may come kicking and not believing with a scream of demons, but deep down you will have the epiphany moment when all is calmer and clearer. I did.

My moment was one late Saturday night I started binge watching Gone with the Wind, North and South, Blue & Grey & Scarlett. That night and most of the next day was so nice, setting at my quilt frame, quilting while watching some of my favorite movies.

Then a moment of calm washed over me like I had been freed of my fears pertaining to the future, the guilt of not knowing could I had done more for him to live, and just simply knowing what to do next. Typically I am the one at the event in control. Through this I thought I had become more peaceful and gained an assurance of what I needed to do in order to be open for what HE had for my widow's walk. After that event I began sleeping through the night and very seldom to this day are held up or woke by those fears anymore. I still have flashbacks when I am awake, of that moment at the end of his life. I guess this is meant to keep me grounded for what is ahead and keep me from returning where I came from.

The next morning I woke up made my morning coffee and started my plan. It was like this was instilled in me through subliminal ways and it was what I was going to go through to survive. It was very organized and clearly understood. That was the morning I actually stepped into my next chapter of life.

I knew the first thing I had to do was go to John's grave and say goodbye. I was not removing him from my soul or heart just ending the grieving drudge to a place that an empty body is entombed. This was to fully let him go, and allow myself to live. I arrived at the cemetery alone shortly after noon. The sun was bright and there wasn't a cloud in the sky. As I arrived near the path leading to John's grave I noticed for the first time a larger than life statue of Jesus in the boat calming the storm. John is only arms away from that beautiful statue. Peace of heart is all I felt at that moment. I spoke out loud to John at his grave as if he was listening and explained what had been happening and that I need to go on to the next chapter in my life. I told him how he would go with me in my heart but I would not be back to this place with him. I left with a little more of the weight lifted off my shoulders. I really didn't feel sad, just calm and at peace and maybe even hopeful of what was to come.

Over the next few weeks I would catch myself asking him out loud "what do you think about….?" Usually this happened on things we always made decisions on together. His presence in the house was a very real feeling at that time. This too seemed to pass as time trudged on.

Now in the first six months after his death I know now I was not in control, I was a mess. I tell you this because as I had so many days and nights worrying about finances and my financial future I made grave financial errors at the advice of what seemed as well-intentioned friends.

The first mistake was I was told my car and truck were getting to much age on them and I needed more reliable transportation. My car was an old classic 1989 Lincoln Town Car and John's truck was a 5 year old Dodge. I was driving over 40 miles to work daily each way and a newer car was enticing. So I did it on January 3rd the next year after his death. I didn't trade in any of the vehicles toward the new one, just went in no money down and drove home in a new car with payments of over $400.00 per month. My girlfriend assured me that I could make the payments and not to worry that I always landed on my feet. This did open up a path to service to another. An lady who became an employee of mine a year or so later had been walking over 10 miles to work and was never late. I gifted her the Lincoln Town Car. She was so proud of that car and treated it like it was brand new. A path of service to others was beginning. I just didn't know it at the time.

Then in April that same year my friend needed a place to live and wanted me to sell her an acre of land so her family could have a permanent place to homestead. Worse 2nd mistake I ever made. As well as the 3rd mistake that was to come soon after with her advice. I don't think she really meant harm then, but later I questioned the overall intentions by using my weak state of mind to benefit them.

John and I had bought a cheap mobile home right after we bought the land and had put it on the property because we had made plans to build a beautiful log cabin in five years or so. Before he got sick we had the floor plans drawn, the logs ready to order and pay for at the mill in Montana. We just needed a little more time to get the cash up for the foundation, plumbing and everything else. Our dream was the house was to be paid for when we turned the key to walk in and to be totally off the grid. It was going to be completely solar powered, geo thermal cooled/heated, private well water and the works.

This well-meaning friend knew there was a few problems with the mobile home there and suggested since I wasn't "skilled" enough to repair them it would be best to just upgrade to a modular home. Her thoughts were that the older small mobile home wasn't safe enough for a woman alone in the country.

This was BIG MISTAKE #3. I met her and her husband at the dealer and fell in love with a large 3 bedroom 2 bath modular home with a wraparound porch, fireplace, and garden tub, recessed lighting large open style kitchen, vaulted ceilings with crown molding. After listening to the sales man's pitch and her advice I put the money down, ordered the house and by June was in debt over my head for a house and property that would never appraise more than the debt. It was 2007 real estate valuations were higher than actual sellable prices. Real Estate was in a "bubble" I would learn later.

Modular homes are beautiful but they are still classified in the real estate world as mobile homes. Therefore they tend to lose value rather than gain. I did not know this at the time, and this was not disclosed to me by the selling entity. If you get nothing else from my writings get this "DO NOT MAKE ANY LIFE CHANGING FINANCIAL DECISIONS IN THE FIRST 12-24 MONTHS". I did and these have haunted me to the date I am writing this book.

So in less than a year or so I added to my grief and debt over $200,000.00 and $1500.00 per month expenses from the ill advice of people close to me.

# CHAPTER FOUR – LIFE WITHOUT OTHERS

As I started getting independent again I learned as a widow the friends you had as a couple are not really your friends anymore. I would call just to talk, no answer, no return calls. Greeting cards sent as usual, none sent back on the next holiday. Then the creepy things started. Some of the men that where his "past" friends" began hitting on me, while others stayed clear not even to acknowledge me when passing in the grocery store or gas station. It made me feel like I had a plague or something. Want your ego to drop even lower, experience this.

As a young widow I found the deacons of the church ignore you too. I guess the commandment to the church to take care of the widows and orphans only apply to the older widows.

My new path led me to the desire to be of service to others. I felt like I was called to serve others and of course it helped with the loneliness. I look back and know I went at this with a bit too much zeal but it is what it was.

The first ministry to others was my love to quilt. I started making lap quilts with a prayer said over them and a verse accompanying them to be given out by the women's ministry when they visited members in the hospital or nursing homes. I also joined the bus ministry at church and loved helping others get to church and driving the seniors to events around Texas. I loved taking the senior members of the church to events like the State Fair and musicals in the hill country. This came to an end when I was told by members of the office staff there was a couple I was not to give a ride to anymore. This couple had mental deficits but was a great help on the bus with our elder passengers. They were a sweet loving couple that was screaming for guidance, help and a loving church home. I know from where I picked them up they were struggling financially and the "system" had failed them. I still deeply believe no person in a church should attempt to stop others from seeking the Lord's house.

This couple would walk in rain and snow the 2 miles to church anyway. I would pass them in the bus and it affected me deeply about this directive I had been given. After this directive that was when I decided that the bus ministry was not for me, at that church. If a congregation cannot accept someone where they are on their path in life, then the congregation needs to look at it's real purpose in the community. I then joined the church choir for special events. But this to waned when I realized a church that turns down followers of the Lord let alone church directors who allow it is not who I can be a part of.

Still seeking that next happy chapter in life I started thinking about taking a leap of faith out of the corporate world. I did take the leap of faith in my life and left the corporate world in March 2010. When I did that, little did I know that my true calling would be revealed!

# CHAPTER FIVE – BUSINESS OWNER-YEAR 4

By this time I had all I could take of sanctimonies back stabbing corporate people's ways. I spent a lot of sleepless nights praying thinking planning studying and researching being a small business owner in Texas. My tolerance for others who did not give 100% on the job was over. My frame of mind to this day has a hard time dealing with lack of character, honesty, and accountability that has become the norm in the world.

There were a lot of things to consider and this is not the path for the weak. There are a lot of long hours, worry, speculations, studying, learner's curves and sheer determination. I still to this day are not bothered by the long hours, it keeps my mind from being idle. There were others even in my own family that did not expect or believe or even want me to succeed, I felt. Every time I would talk to them on my successes they would always change the conversation to some other family members businesses or career successes. Never saying, wow you are doing good! Instead I received statements like, "Are you really making money?" This to date still bothers me of their lack of conviction to my business or well being.

March 2010 I had had enough, I gave my notice at work and within the month I was on my way to opening my own business. This was year four of my walk. For me this freedom of mind has been liberating. It allowed me the option to go to college at night for a degree all the while learning the small business world. This knowledge gave me the determination and wisdom to follow my God driven path.

My path was and is to this day to help Veterans, Widows, and others left behind live through this part of life. I assist them and advise them from what I have lived through to a path towards their earned benefits, pensions and more. It amazes me every day how these earned benefits are a mystery to the majority. Benefits like service connected illnesses that could help with their financial bottom line on many levels. I have spoken to various benefit coordinators at the VA regional offices; they have told me so many times how many widows do not know what Veteran recourses are available to them.

Through this path of training and advising I was implemental in starting a grass roots movement in our area to help homeless Veterans off the streets and back to the farm. Statistics reveal that

54% of all Veterans come from a rural background. Through this model they would do the day to day chores of handling animals, planting and enjoying what they grew up with. This style hands on regimented demands helps them get back to who they were and it helped me to get over the trauma we have both faced in our past. This movement went on with me collaborating locally to write a course that was received well by the local college agriculture department. This course was a step by step retraining into a sustainable small farm business. Most agriculture models are taught on large scale truck farm practices.

This model was different from all the others you here about today. It not only gave each Veteran or their Widows the ability to earn an accredited well rounded college degree, but it gave them a close network of others who have been where they have been to lean on, mentor, and grow with. Kind of like an intended family.

Most degrees once earned put you out in the real world alone; this is not what we needed. I went on to develop a cooperative of Veterans who were already growing small to be another support mechanism for the younger Veterans and Widows going through this course. To date there has been some setbacks in getting the curriculum on schedule. And the setbacks started from the untimely death of the Ag Director, to the changing of the Dean a few times. One of the Veterans who was on the board of the coop and who is now teaching at that local college has taken the helm to get the facility and curriculum on track. As to small farm model I wrote for the local college and how I came to that place, John and I had always talked about a startup small farm business and we both had the sixth sense that our plot of land could help us, and others all the while making us a living. We didn't seek to be rich just sustainable.

To this day I have personally helped many Veterans get service connected paperwork filled out and helped widows to learn what is there for them and their paperwork. I love researching and helping most everyone I have encountered, as long as they are respectful of my efforts.

As I reflect back on events and where I have come to today, I had to go through life with and after John to get to where I could serve others. Personally I would have preferred a seminar or course but maybe my passion would not have been in the right place. Who knows!

My new business did not start with a farm it started seeking out local Veteran growers and opening an indoor local food market. I did get into the fresh egg production business and can tell you hens are the best pets for making the worries of the world slip away. When I spent time just sitting there watching them go through their pecking order trials, and just their daily lives a lot of the grief and despair would just fade away. Hens were my therapy pets.

My little indoor local food market took off so quick I, as a new business owner doing this all alone, was so overwhelmed. I opened it in a market off US Hwy 287 in a rural area. I did this so it would not grow so fast that I couldn't manage it myself and so that I could learn the business, gain more contacts, and start my own production models. But those first six months just about killed me physically. The demand required I travel further out to more local small farms. I guess my due diligence paid off. In an area where the population was less than 40,000 people in a 50 mile radius the produce flew off the shelves. Then I expanded by the end of the first year. I added local farm fresh dairy, opened a deli side so that I could make and teach about making my jarred jellies, homemade butter, cheese and pies.

I have gone into detail here because by now I was getting restless. Not wanting to end the business venture but lonely for someone to talk to. My girlfriends were not as available once I was a business owner. I guess I was very busy but just answering a simple text or phone call wasn't that hard, or so I thought. I always made time for them in their time of need.

This business rocked on and the next year came (year 5). I was teaching a class of how to make homemade pickles to a group in the deli area of the store and this fellow walked in. He looked over the jarred goods and chose a jar of Homemade Peach Cobbler, paid and left.

# CHAPTER SIX- YEAR 6

This tall whitehead quiet man, would come into my market on Saturday mornings, and pick up a few things but always a jelly or jarred dessert. We didn't initially have much time to talk because at that time I was teaching canning classes, but he did start coming in more often over the next year.

He seemed gentle but very reserved and I was drawn to him like a moth to a flame, I guess.

As that year flew by he came around more often until one day he was gone. He didn't show back up for three months and only came in for a quick snack and left again. Later that year he came in during one of my canning classes and kind of hung around a bit, we talked like old friends and there began a budding relationship with another widow. We both had somewhat common ground by being widowed. Looking back I think that was an ice breaker for both of us to open up to someone else.

When days were slow at the market we would sit on the front porch and talk. Relating our stories of loss, children, work past etc. Before too long we knew enough about each other that our friendship seemed like it had been lifelong.

A funny path and event started to unfold. He rode with me one very early morning to pick up and deliver from and to the local farms. On this ride he revealed before he was drafted into the Vietnam Conflict he worked his summers on a farm in Michigan. He had also been growing produce where he and his late wife had lived with success, especially when it came to black eyed peas. Right up my alley so to speak. I was into Veterans farming and selling for them. At the time he was wandering trying to find where he wanted to start his next chapter of life. He had bought an RV and though about traveling but going alone, didn't seem to settle him. Not too long after the first mornings farm trip, we started the talk of him moving up to my farm and planting as much as we could to supplement the areas where I had to seek produce. This would help with cutting down on the mileage and more.

And so our lives evolved and two lone widowers were not lonely anymore! Though we are just friends over the next 3 years our friendship grew tight and we grew enough produce to support twelve customers families with weekly boxes of fresh produce as well as fill in where other growers couldn't. It was a financial win for the business but a back braking physically hard path for both of us.

I look back and I believe it helped us work through the stress and maybe deep sorrow of our losses and changes to our path we didn't want to happen. It also gave us stable thinking time, which after a loss like this you must have!

As drought crept in over the next year we had to seek other ways to make the business sustain. I was already dabbling in the online selling environment, but didn't have the assets to invest heavy into a sellable product. My business started to change towards others unwanted assets and looking back we help so many more people than just the Veterans now through online and event sales.

The evolution started with me taking on consignments to sell for others, while he ran the produce side. Things people did not want anymore that still had value, and things people were left with from estates and more where brought to me to sell for them. Over the next few years this computer selling valet service turned into full house estates. The local postal carriers were not happy when they had full truck loads to haul from just us. More burdens were lifted from those left with large life collections. What a joy it is to package them up and see them headed out!.
Think you don't come full circle in life. Watch out for the ride!

At this time I still had all John's dad's stuff, John's stuff and he had his entire late wife's life collections. These are things that are a burden to keep, store and move. These are things that bring back memories and pain. I think of a passage in the bible that says "you come from your mother's womb naked, and as everyone comes, so they depart. They take nothing from their toil that they can carry in their hands."

While I was selling other peoples burdens, I started the downsizing of our burdens. It took me a year to liquidate the excess and with him helping me we scaled down to what would fit in an RV!

Eight years had passed by then and the produce stand was closed, that portion of the business handed over to the local farms we sourced from and we moved the business into helping more people get rid of material objects through my skill in sales. The local food movement is in good hands and still thriving.

To date we have liquidated small estates, as well as hoarders estates and enjoy seeing the burden lifted off our clients when they come back and the house is completely empty, what a joyous day! This path of our journey has helped us both heal in ways no counselling could ever have done. We know now that our path side by side is to help heal others and lift them from the burden of materialism.

Life is a fickle road. You think you know where and who you will end up living your days out with, then in the snap of a finger things will change. A simple word, an action or even a reaction can change your walk in ways that will forever affect you.

In life we don't have the answers. That's why the old Christian song says 'we will know in the by and by". It is true when your mind is ready things are revealed to you.

You may think you know where you are going, but let me tell you from experience, YOU DON'T! In a blink of an eye your comfortable life can change and throw you out of your comfort zone, like a tornado does to a house.

Listen to that voice in your head that is steering you down a better path, just be still, and listen.
Your innermost thoughts will be your guiding force for your future.

# ABOUT THE AUTHOR

I am Southern Christian women born under the sign of Leo. As I write, I pray that my ramblings will help someone else along their way. Widowed at 45 years old and I am still wandering this old world helping others down the path I have already had to travel.

52190014R00020